BOOKWORMS

Migrating Animals

Sharks

Arthur Best

Cavendish Square
New York

Published in 2019 by Cavendish Square Publishing, LLC
243 5th Avenue, Suite 136, New York, NY 10016

First Edition

Library of Congress Cataloging-in-Publication Data

Names: Best, B. J., 1976- author.
Title: Sharks / Arthur Best.
Description: First edition. | New York : Cavendish Square, 2019. | Series:
Migrating animals | Audience: Grades K-2. | Includes index. |
Identifiers: LCCN 2017052044 (print) | LCCN 2017054740 (ebook) | ISBN
9781502637185 (ebook) | ISBN 9781502637178 (library bound) | ISBN
9781502637192 (pbk.) | ISBN 9781502637208 (6 pack)
Subjects: LCSH: Sharks--Juvenile literature. | Migratory animals--Juvenile literature.
Classification: LCC QL638.9 (ebook) | LCC QL638.9 .B476 2019 (print) | DDC 597.3/4--dc23
LC record available at https://lccn.loc.gov/2017052044

Editorial Director: David McNamara
Copy Editor: Nathan Heidelberger
Associate Art Director: Amy Greenan
Designer: Megan Metté
Production Coordinator: Karol Szymczuk
Photo Research: J8 Media

The photographs in this book are used by permission and through the courtesy of: Cover Wildest Animal/Shuterstock.com; p. 5, 15 Reinhard Dirscherl/Ullstein Bild/Getty Images; p. 07 Richard Robinson/Cultura/Getty Images; p. 9 Antonio Busiello/Robert Harding/Getty Images; p. 11 Alexander Safonov/Moment Select/ Getty Images; p. 13 Vincent Truchet/Biosphoto/Getty Images; p. 17 Auscape/UIG/Getty Images; p. 19 Fedor Selivanov/Alamy Stock Photo; p. 21 Water Frame/ Alamy Stock Photo.

Printed in the United States of America

Contents

Sharks live in the sea.

They are big.

Sharks have soft bones.

But they are strong!

They can swim fast.

Sharks eat **plankton**.

Sharks eat crabs.

Sharks eat fish.

Sharks like good water.

The water can't be too cold.

It can't be too warm.

Sharks **migrate**.

They can swim far.

Sharks migrate to find food.

They migrate to find
good water.

A **blacktip** is a kind of shark.

It has black on its top **fin**.

Blacktips migrate to have babies.

A baby shark is called a **pup**.

The pups grow.

Soon they will migrate too!

New Words

blacktip (BLAK-tip) A kind of shark.

fin (FIN) A body part of a shark that helps it swim.

migrate (MY-grate) To travel far to live in a new place.

plankton (PLANK-tun) Small plants and animals in the sea.

pup (PUP) Baby shark.

Index

About the Author

Arthur Best lives in Wisconsin with his wife and son. He has written many other books for children. He has seen a shark in Hawaii.

About BOOKWORMS

Bookworms help independent readers gain reading confidence through high-frequency words, simple sentences, and strong picture/text support. Each book explores a concept that helps children relate what they read to the world they live in.